Nature Basics

Solids, Liquids, and Gases

by Carol K. Lindeen

Consulting Editor: Gail Saunders-Smith, PhD

Consultant: Sandra Mather, PhD
Professor Emerita of Geology and Astronomy
West Chester University, Pennsylvania

Capstone
press®

Mankato, Minnesota

Pebble Books are published by Capstone Press,
151 Good Counsel Drive, P.O. Box 669, Mankato, Minnesota 56002.
www.capstonepress.com

1 2 3 4 5 6 12 11 10 09 08 07

Library of Congress Cataloging-in-Publication Data
Lindeen, Carol, 1976–
    Solids, liquids, and gases / by Carol K. Lindeen.
        p. cm.—(Pebble Books. Nature basics)
    Includes bibliographical references and index.
    ISBN-13: 978-1-4296-0002-6 (hardcover)
    ISBN-10: 1-4296-0002-0 (hardcover)
    ISBN-13: 978-1-4296-2892-1 (softcover pbk.)
    ISBN-10: 1-4296-2892-8 (softcover pbk.)
    1. Solids—Juvenile literature. 2. Liquids—Juvenile literature. 3. Gas—Juvenile
literature. 4. Matter—Properties—Juvenile literature. I. Title. II. Series.
QC176.3.L56 2008
530.4—dc22   2006101957

Summary: Simple text and photographs present solids, liquids, and gases.

Note to Parents and Teachers

The Nature Basics set supports national science standards related
to earth and life science. This book describes and illustrates
solids, liquids, and gases. The images support early readers in
understanding the text. The repetition of words and phrases helps
early readers learn new words. This book also introduces early
readers to subject-specific vocabulary words, which are defined
in the Glossary section. Early readers may need assistance to read
some words and to use the Table of Contents, Glossary, Read More,
Internet Sites, and Index sections of the book.

Table of Contents

Matter

Look around.

Everything you see is matter.

Air is matter too.

Matter can be
a solid, liquid, or gas.

Solids

Solids have their
own shape.
Solids are hard or soft.
Trees are hard.
Their leaves are soft.

8

Some solids melt
into liquids.
Icicles melt on
a sunny day.

Liquids

Liquids don't have
their own shape.
Rain fills up a pond.

Liquids can freeze
and become solid.
Pond water freezes
in winter.

Gases

Gases have no shape.
Air is made of gases.
We feel these gases
when the wind blows.

16

Boiling water
turns into a gas.
Steam rises
from a pot as gas.

Gases inside balloons
make them rise
into the air.

Matter is everywhere.
What solids, liquids,
and gases are
around you?

Glossary

freeze—to change from a liquid to a solid

gas—matter that has no shape and spreads to fill any space that holds it

liquid—something wet that takes the shape of whatever holds it; liquids can be poured.

melt—to change from a solid to a liquid

solid—matter that has its own shape

steam—gas that forms when water boils

Read More

Ballard, Carol. *Solids, Liquids, and Gases: From Ice Cubes to Bubbles.* Science Answers. Chicago: Heinemann Library, 2004.

Stille, Darlene. *Matter: See It, Touch It, Taste It, Smell It.* Amazing Science. Minneapolis: Picture Window Books, 2004.

Internet Sites

FactHound offers a safe, fun way to find Internet sites related to this book. All of the sites on FactHound have been researched by our staff.

Here's how:

1. Visit *www.facthound.com*
2. Choose your grade level.
3. Type in this book ID **1429600020** for age-appropriate sites. You may also browse subjects by clicking on letters, or by clicking on pictures and words.
4. Click on the **Fetch It** button.

FactHound will fetch the best sites for you!

Index

Word Count: 119
Grade: 1
Early-Intervention Level: 14

Editorial Credits
Erika L. Shores, editor; Ted Williams, designer; Jo Miller, photo researcher;
    Kelly Garvin, photo stylist

Photo Credits
Bruce Coleman Inc./Daniel Dempster, 14
Capstone Press/Karon Dubke, 16
Dreamstime/Brad Thompson, 18; Sheena Koontz, 1
fotolia/Eric Limon, 20; Igor V, 6; podius, 8
iStockphoto/Jacom Stephens, 4; Joop Snijder, 12
Shutterstock/Elemental Imaging, cover (balloon); July Flower, 10; Tischenko Irina,
    cover (glass)